ox 394

D1824173

MACDOG'S HOME

By Caroline and John Astrop

Crocodile

Your nest looks cosy.

May I try it?

It's very high

and too prickly.

Where do bees live?

I can't get in there.

Frog's home floats.

Oh dear, I'm too heavy.

Do chickens have a home?

This is too silly.

Where do you live squirrel?

Follow me!

Trees again.

Help! I'm slipping.

Rabbit, your home looks fun.

Oh, it's too tight.

Where do foxes live?

I won't try another hole in the ground.

I think the best home

is mine.

Where do these animals live?

Have you seen their homes?